I Speak of Simple Things

DONNA G. HUMPHREY

AMP&RSAND, INC.

Chicago, Illinois

First Edition–September 2007
Second Edition–November 2007
ISBN 978-09761235-7-6

Book Design: David Robson, Robson Design

Published by Ampersand, Inc.
1050 N. State St., Chicago, IL 60610
Suzanne T. Isaacs, Publisher
www.ampersandworks.com

Printed in the United States of America

To the strong and noble women of the prairie.

ACKNOWLEDGMENTS

Kathleen Kennedy and Mary Schmich, who have a poet's heart, inspired us to go forward. Suzanne Isaacs, who fell in love with the project, gave us the courage.

Helena Lefkow patiently organized the original material and typed the copy. Laura Lefkow assisted in locating and editing photographs. *The Ancestors and Descendants of Alexander Walker Glenn and Nancy Austin*, compiled by Gene B. Foss and Iona Spencer (1973), was an invaluable source of Glenn family history.

Despite our desire to remain true to the original texts, Donna was not a good typist. She would be the first to tell you. To assist our readers, we took some editorial liberty by occasionally inserting a comma, deleting a period, or making similar minor changes. We did our best not to change the flow or the meaning. We also added titles to the following untitled poems: "A Pattern On the Floor," "But, God, I Hurt," "Life Savings" (originally titled "Old Woman"), "So Long Ago," "Wish," "Today In a Quiet Church," "Bondage," and "The Way." A number of the poems have several versions. We chose the version we liked best.

J.H.L.

J.H.S.

Donna with Joan, John, Judy and Tim,
their much loved collie-shepherd, 1945.

AN INTRODUCTION

DONNA GRACE GLENN HUMPHREY was born in Nemaha County, Kansas, on August 25, 1915, the fourth child of Coloma Jane Record and Hugh Ashley Glenn.

The Glenns moved west from Pennsylvania through Kentucky during the era of Daniel Boone. Donna's great-great-grandfather was Alexander Walker Glenn, a farmer who married Nancy Austin in 1829 and settled in Boone County, Missouri. In 1855 the Glenns moved to Lecompton, Kansas, and were among the earliest pioneers settling the Kansas Territory.

According to family lore, one of Alexander and Nancy Glenn's sons, Hugh Thomas, left his family and went to California, perhaps intending to return, but he died there "of a fever," it was said. His son, John Thomas, at age 13, ran away from a difficult stepfather to live with an uncle in Sabetha, Kansas. He became a farmer in nearby Woodlawn, a small town providing services to the farmers and settlers of the area. John and his wife Sylvia Ermine Ashley—they were known as Tom and Min—had three children; the eldest, Hugh Ashley, was Donna's father. Tom and Min were founding members of the Woodlawn Baptist Church, a faith community in which Donna and her children were brought up and which holds regular services to this day.

Her mother's family, Donna wrote, "was very different from the Glenns." The Records were latecomers to Kansas, "a rather wandering family who had moved from Nebraska, to Missouri, to Iowa, and lately to Kansas." Coloma Jane was the fifth child of nine in the family of Sarah Rachel and Robert Allen

I SPEAK OF SIMPLE THINGS

Record. "Al Record was illiterate but was an accomplished carpenter and, as such, he provided after a fashion for his enormous brood," Donna said. "[Coloma] brought from her single days a fine sewing machine. She had been a seamstress before she married. She had bought the machine with her own money and prized it highly." She was a comely woman with beautiful hair.

According to Donna, Coloma fell in love when she met Hugh Glenn. They were married in 1909. Like Tom and Min, Hugh and Coloma also farmed near Woodlawn. From all accounts, the romance did not endure. Hugh was jealous of his wife, emotionally distant, harsh with the children, and family life was grim. A son, Willis, died at age 11. Coloma's health failed. There was too much work, too much sadness and despair. As Donna put it, "We were emotionally impoverished by a lack of love, laughter, trust, and just simple fun, which was poverty indeed."

Donna described her grandmother Min as the one person in her childhood who tried to bring a bit of joy into her life, with small gifts and books. Min enrolled her in a correspondence school after Donna's father closed the door on her plan to go to high school. She was needed at home to care for her ill mother and the young family. Donna may have started the correspondence course; she never spoke of it, so it is unlikely she finished more than a course or two.

At 17, Donna began seeing a handsome young man, Otis L. "Jake" Humphrey, the son of Kentucky emigrants to Woodlawn. They were married October 6, 1933. During the Great Depression, they moved with their young son, John, to Denver in pursuit of work but, failing to get a foothold, they returned within a couple of years to farm 480 acres near Woodlawn. John recalls that they bought a 1933 Plymouth coupe with a rumble seat for the return trip.

Jake and Donna reared their four children on the farm until, in 1954, they sold part of their land and purchased and ran a general store in Woodlawn. The Woodlawn General Store was the last commercial enterprise in Woodlawn as, by this time, it had dwindled to a crossroads.

They closed the store in 1958. Jake, who had begun building houses for neighbors, built a new house for his family on the farm where Donna was born and which is the subject of "Leavetaking." The leavetaking occurred in 1960 when the family sold the farm and moved to Sabetha.

Actualizing a dream of having money to call her own, Donna got her first job in an office after composing a letter of application so exceptional that her employer selected her over women with office experience. In 1964, Jake and Donna returned to Denver. Donna worked for many years at a hospital, retiring as assistant to the controller in the late 1970s. Jake died in 1977 and Donna lived alone as a widow for nearly 30 years.

Donna suffered from chronic depression, bearing feelings she identified as "losses, humiliations, longings unfulfilled, unnameable yearnings, and most of all, that hideous, nearly unbearable knowledge of failure." Under such clouds, her young married children announced each pregnancy knowing that it would not necessarily be good news to her. She dwelt on the emotional pain of her past which must have equaled the terrible pain and humiliation she endured as a result of a genetic malformation of her feet. Without treatments widely available now, she groped through her darkness by reading her Bible and praying to a God by whom she often felt abandoned. Yet through her faith, determination (see "Small Beginnings"), and the love and responsibility she felt for her children, she endured and in many respects thrived to do her duty to husband, family, and community.

In another era, Donna would have had a different life. This intelligent, sensitive woman would certainly have gone to high school! Her depression and disability might have been managed better. We can only imagine what might have been. She lived with what was and so do we.

Later in life, those feared-for grandchildren became perhaps Donna's greatest enjoyment. With them she could unbridle her love and let it flow. Food was important. She called it "just country cooking," but each grandchild treasures the memory of being welcomed to her home by a cherry pie or cinnamon rolls freshly baked just for them. She hand made a patchwork quilt for each; the last for her great-grandson John remains in tiny pieces, unfinished. Her grandson, Glen Kauffman, at her funeral stated, "I celebrate my grandmother's life, her love of words, her passion for spirituality, her fervent opinions on politics. She was born of that strong and noble Kansas farmer blood, growing up in a time that her grandchildren cannot begin to appreciate. She devoted her life to ensure a better future for us. Grandma found and filled a gap in each of our lives. We were blessed by her ability to make each one of us feel like number one."

At some time—probably while quite young—Donna began to write poetry. A clue is found in a memory book where Laura asked her grandmother to "[s]hare a memory involving an outhouse." Donna answered, "I wrote my first poem, standing at the door of the outhouse watching the snow fall—the first snow of the season. I wrote:

Little fairy snowflakes falling
Falling through the air…

and on and on." She added, "Not great immortal words but after that I wrote lots of verses."

We know that she wrote poems as a young mother. A few were published in *The Poetry Forum* during the 1950s. She also wrote a winning jingle for a cleaning product for which she won a gold watch, a great thrill for a woman for whom new clothes and jewelry were only fantasy. Occasionally, over the years, other poems were published but most were shared one at a time with a daughter, niece, or trusted friend, then tucked away in drawers and in closets safe from the fearsome criticism that warped her sense of self as a child (see "The Watcher").

Donna died a horrifying death on February 28, 2005 at the age of 89 while visiting with her daughter Joan and family in Chicago. The event was widely covered by the media and will not be dignified by description in these pages. Because she was an aged woman, the loss of Donna was eclipsed by the death at the same time of her son-in-law, Michael Lefkow, and the outpouring of sympathy to his wife and young daughters. A few friends who knew of Donna's poetry, however, asked at that time to receive a copy of her work. These requests were the seed planted in our minds and hearts that led us to publish this collection of the poems we discovered as we sifted through her things that winter and the following spring.

Those who knew her well knew she had a keen sense of humor, distaste for falsity, and uncommon intelligence. In publishing her poems we present our mother as she was, "all wool and a yard wide," as she liked to say. Would she have approved of making this collection public? We are confident that she would have, even though a few reveal secrets she did not share outside her intimate circle. To hold these back would have distorted the truth of her life.

Primarily, it is a gift to our children and our children's children, to the end of Donna's line, so that they may know this grandmother, who was an extraordinary woman. And we hope that all who read her verses will see in her verbal images an era now past of rural life, unromantic, often cruel, its harshness smoothed by the wonder of the natural world, the communion of family, and the yearning we know as God.

Joan Humphrey Lefkow · Judith Humphrey Smith
August, 2007

CONTENTS

LONGING

FAMILY

THE WORLD OUTSIDE

FAITH AND PRAYER

Donna Grace Glenn
at four months.

IF I WERE A POET

If I were a poet
I could speak my thoughts in language
All sublime and terrible. Perhaps
My words would span my generation:
Children, yet unborn, might strive
To plumb their meaning.
But I, I only know of simple things:
Heart-stabbing winter sunsets,
The unexpected thrust of pain
That tells me life is fragile,
That moments such as this
In which the western sky pours glory
On a snowy cornfield are significant.
I speak of ordinary things: of wind-swept fields,
Of bright May mornings when my wash is hung
To dry in breezes sweetened by the apple blossoms
On the tree my father planted.
My thoughts are not profound:
I only speak of simple things.

TWILIGHT STORY

Some wandering rays from the setting sun
Played late in the mulberry, cool,
Got caught in the branches and slipped and fell
Right into the orchard pool;
And they might have drowned, but Lady Dark
Saw them there as she drifted past
Pulled them out with the help of Evening Star
Who guided them home at last!

Written between 1964 and 1975

*Farm near Woodlawn, Kansas where the Humphrey family lived
from 1939 to 1954.*

I SPEAK OF SIMPLE THINGS

THANKS-GIVING

I thank You, God, for all these ordinary things;
For water that flows freely from the faucet to my tub
Or drawn from wells by windmills to the tanks
Where thirsty horses drink and drink
And shake their thankful heads and drink again.

I thank You for the wheatfields waving gently
In the wind, ripe for the reaping;
Golden in the fields and golden in the bread
Upon my table.

Thank You for the prairie grasses
Red and gold in Autumn
Dying in a blaze of glory—so it seems—
But then, come April, they are richly green
Nourishing the bison, then the cattle
When the buffalo are gone.
These grasses came by Nature's providence
Bursting, as it were, unsummoned
From the Prairie-Erth.

Thank You, too, for the forests; trees
That drop their leaves in Autumn on the earth
To give it nourishment; for logs in fireplaces
Where we warm ourselves and sometimes see our dreams
Go up in flames and die; For Christmas trees—
And for the lonely beam from which we made a cross
And hanged the Man who made it all!
But like the earth in Spring, Life does not die!
The Author lives! I thank You, God,
For all these "ordinary" things!

SUMMER STORM

They looked out on the field of corn
Where, just this morning, Hope stood, dark green
And shoulder high. They saw it through a blur
Of steam and mist as wind and rain and hail
Combined to wreak a senseless fury
On the green and innocent promise
Of the fields.
Silently they watched. The roar of storm so loud
To drown the sound of speaking.
Silently, they waited for the storm to pass.

Gradually the roar became a murmur, then a drip
Of an occasional raindrop on the roof,
And then, as though nothing at all had happened
The sun broke through and cast a shining rainbow
On the dark and hurrying cloud.
The man pulled on his boots, she made no move to go;
This was his time to be alone. She watched him
As he slowly slogged his way through all that muddy waste
Where, just this morning, Hope stood, shoulder high.
Returning to the house (which held his riches, after all)
He grinned a little wryly as he said, "The Lord giveth,
And the Lord taketh away." She smiled and touched his hand.
"And blessed is His name," she answered.

Donna and Jake Humphrey, 1940s.

I SPEAK OF SIMPLE THINGS

PARABLE ON SPARROWS

The snow came in the night
And covered every weed and blade of grass
And so, this morning, in a little pan
I poured out seed to feed the birds
And did a land-office business
In sparrows. "Those greedy birds,"
I thought, "They're hardly worth the saving!
They drive the better birds away,
With all their noise and numbers,
And what a mess they make!"
And then, I thought, "God cares for sparrows,
'Marks their fall!' and if He does,
I guess I ought." And so
I poured a bit more seed out in the pan
And pondered on the ways of God
With sparrows, and with man.

Written between 1988 and 2004

SUNRISE

The rising sun glares through my windshield
Brutally, blinding me. Frantically
I strain to see some guiding line
Against the morning traffic.
A phrase I read this morning speaks,
"Give thanks for everything!
This is My will concerning you."

Grimly, angrily, I acquiesce: "O.K., Lord,
Thank You for that—sun!"
Then I thought,
"God, thank You for that sun! Without it,
this would be a frozen ball of death
hurtling through space!"

Your light is like the sun;
Your unrelenting brilliance
Makes me long for some small shade
In which to hide, and yet,
Outside the light, I die!

Written in 1975; published in New Zealandia, *1995*

A PATTERN ON THE FLOOR

Grandma spoke into the phone. "They say
She can't live through the night."
"She" was my mother and I heard the words,
The words I still remember and my Grandma's
Tall, spare frame, the window and the pattern
Of the sun on Grandma's floor. That is all.
I was eight. My mother was the only light I knew
And yet I don't remember fear or pain or grief…nothing
But my Grandma's form, the sun that made
A pattern on the floor and my own small self
Standing in the doorway.

Written between 1988 and 2004

Donna's mother, Coloma Jane Glenn, age 20.
An accomplished seamstress, Coloma made this
beautiful suit as well as the dramatic hat.

BILL (CIRCA 1920–1930)

I have small certainties about the ways of God
But some child-minded angel
Must have touched my father's heart so that
He bid upon and bought
A leggy, lovely saddle horse named "Bill."

Embarrassed by his rank extravagance
(No plow-horse, this!) he brought him home.
My brothers led him out, gravely covering their joy
With manly objectivity (too much exuberance
Would never do). One by one they tried him out
And found his gait as smooth as silk and given rein
That horse would all but fly!

I was too young (a girl!) to ride alone
But came a day when I could lift the saddle,
Cinch it tight, and climbing up,
Begin my tentative steps to freedom.
And came another day and days when girl and horse
Beyond the sight of elders, streaked through pastures,
Jumping ditches, risking life and bones
At breakneck speed and then, sedately, home again,
Bringing the cows for milking.
This one sweet, happy memory, almost unchanged
By time, I carry from my Kansas childhood;
This one delight: My friendship
With a leggy, lovely saddle horse named "Bill."

SMALL BEGINNINGS

…"Can't never make
A silk purse from a sow's ear!"
My grandmother's words with sharp, sardonic laughter
Echoed in my mind as I, bare, muddy feet
Curled 'round the rails of the hog-yard fence,
Fixed my attention on those sows
(Surely Nature's most unlovely)
Wallowing sensuously in the cooling mud.

Instinctively I knew my place in Grandma's barbed
Analogy. Inwardly rebelling, silently protesting,
Contemptuously I watched those sows
Grunting sleepily, contented in the sun
While one small farmer's daughter's fiercely angry tears
Fell on the hog-yard fence. Somehow in my childish
Consciousness the goal was set.
"Maybe I can't! Maybe it can't be done!
But I will never know, for I will die
Still trying!"

Donna's grandmother,
"Min" Glenn, August 9, 1942,
dressed for her son
James' wedding.

FRUSTRATION

I long to be a poet; and once, I thought I would.
I'd write of love and life and stuff
As no one else quite could.
And so I wrote my patient lines
I bared my secret soul;
Poured out my heart in anguished words,
Sure that I'd reach my goal
Of published works and public praise;
But now, at long, sad last
I know the truth: it shall not be.
No verse of mine shall cast
Its deathless spell on future minds
In near and distant lands.
I simply cannot say a thing so no one understands.
My meaning's clear, in black and white,
So anyone may know it;
And so, I know for certain, sure,
I'll never be a poet!

As published in The Poetry Forum, *April 5, 1959*

LINES FROM
THE BLUE NOTEBOOK

Planted, she was
In arid soil of poverty and neglect.
Fourth in line; wild, unnurtured,
Not love enough for four.
Hardly for one.
Guilty she was; guilty of being
A child. Guilty
Of hating the work, the poverty of spirit.
Guilty for being.
Graceless she grew
Sturdy; a weed, she blossomed.
Rounded, wanted, not understanding;
Needing, for promise of love,
She married.
Fecund, she was;
Coupling, she brought forth children;
Loving, learning, growing old,
Living, dying.
Life.

CHOICE

We'd had a child, our third, in January
Then, our fourth in February next.

"At last, it's over: no more children.
These four will have my best, but
No more children!"

And then—the old familiar certainty
That here was yet another, begging to be born.

The times were hard. We were hard pressed,
Sick of being sick, furious
That my will had not been done
I took the life beginning.
I murdered him…or her.

Whom did I kill, I wonder.
Four lived. One died.

I wonder when my time shall be no more
Will this child ask me, "Why?"

BUT, GOD, I HURT

Today I'm feeling really bad!
I know that I should trust You in all circumstance
And give You thanks. I know all that.
But, God, I hurt,
Hurt with a pain that does not go away,
A not at all unique kind of pain
And quite the smallest, least significant part
Of all the awful aggregate
Of human suffering.
It would not cause the smallest bit
Of extraordinary comment, should I tell
The reasons (sometimes I tell
The reasons, so I know).
If I'd been singled out for some dramatic,
Job-like misery I might seem
A valiant carrier of woes
And everyone would note
With just a touch of awe, perhaps,
But mine is ordinary, everyday, mundane—
And lonely. Does it end, this pain?

RETROSPECT

I reached for life with greedy hands
Snatched it green from lowest
Branches, then I found
The taste was bitter on my tongue.
And this was just and right, I grant,
Except that those who shared my table
Also shared the bitter fruit.

LIFE SAVINGS

A book unopened in her lap, she rocks
Through eighty years' remembering.
Searching for gold in slag and shale of living
The heart stumbles. Recalling love and its illusion,
Birthing, the heart enlarging with each child,
Hope and promise, failure and despair,
All dim in memory of simple things:
An Autumn bonfire in the meadow,
Flames shooting sparks like fireworks
Through the high-piled hedgebrush;
Or hanging wash to dry on apple-blossom mornings
Fragrant from the trees her father planted;
And bitter-sweet the stab of melancholy
As winter sunsets turned the snowy fields to crimson.
Inconsequential, all of this, but tempering sorrow,
Reducing bitter loss to poignant memory.

The book unopened in her lap, she rocks
And counts her gold in simple things
The heart remembers.

Written between 1988 and 2004

*Donna enjoying herself
at a Central City casino, 2002.*

THE WATCHER

He perched above my little bed, I think,
And whispered to my small, unconscious mind,
"Here lies a proper fool!" and when
The infant consciousness awoke
The message was the only voice it knew.
On my shoulder, in my mind
He never sleeps. He tells me
Of my sins, my failures, and
The foolish ways I've walked,
And I think that on the speaking stone
That tells my name my enemy will perch
Still, still accusing. But at last
I will not hear, I will be free.
I will be free.

Donna's father, Hugh Ashley Glenn.
His wedding portrait, 1909.

LIFE STORY

Take any day at random and you have
A life in miniature. We wake
At dawn, just as an infant child
Begins to be aware of living. The morning hours
Seem long. How prodigally we spend
These golden days of childhood! There's
Time and time to spare, we think;
And noon comes on us unawares. We cast
A thoughtful glance up toward the sun
Recalling all the work that's still undone,
But then, there's still a half-day left.
We hurry on, the hours are flying now
And it's mid-afternoon. A bit chagrined
We face the certainty that much we planned
Will have to be forgotten. More slowly now
We turn our hands to that which matters most.
The evening comes, what's done is done!
We rest a while, the day goes by in retrospect
Our weary thoughts grow more confused;
The night comes softly, softly down.
And so, to sleep.

Written between 1961 and 1964

OF TIME AND LETTERS

There is no time;
For life is day to day and hour to hour
And maybe there will never be tomorrow;
And we have walked with Awful Death so long
That he's become, if not a friend,
At least a boon companion.
Great thoughts take time
And so our presses roll
With light, bright, facile words;
Or dark, sour, evil words;
Brightly or darkly empty, which have passed
This one criterion: Will it sell?
We need men now to think and dream
And build again the stairway to the stars
For our bright, lovely young to climb.
(These young we breed as though we thought
Our world would last forever!)

Written February 23, 1966

*Jake and Donna at home
at 511 North Sixth Street,
Sabetha, Kansas, 1963.*

IN DEFENSE OF MIDDLE AGE

Middle age is not so bad as I've been led to think
In fact, since I've reached forty-five
And frankly on the brink
Of growing really old I find
A certain compensation. There
Are many things that go with youth
That I can freely bear
To lay aside; such as: the female competition
For the male approval! There's a war
In which I gladly hoist the white flag
Of surrender! And it's just as well
For though I tried,
The role of *femme fatale*
Was never quite my line since
Nature left me disadvantaged in that field.
Now is the time for easy clothes and books
And friends whom you have known so long
That how you look is just the last thing they could tell you
If you asked. Now is the time for still, uncluttered rooms
And for the joy of children coming just to visit
Whose mothers take them home after a while.
In middle age you've come to terms with money;
Not that there's a lot but just that years of buying "things"
Has taught at least this wisdom: Life does not consist
In the abundance of possessions. So, with loss
Of youth I find, surprisingly enough,
The gain is greater. We may toss aside the husk of life
And with knowledge gained in youth
Enjoy its savor.

Written in 1960

DENVER: 1938

I'd like to have my Denver back!
A sort of quiet town where for a nickel
You could buy a burger. Street car tracks
Went all the way from here to there
And back again, clattering, sparking on the wires
Certain as the sunrise. Downtown was just
A dime or so away with stores of elegance;
The Denver and The May and D. and F.
(Daniels and Fisher to you!) The clerks
Wore black with just a touch of white (and heels!)
Sometimes we'd have our lunch up in the Tea Room
At The Denver for a treat.
And Denver ended just at Sheridan on the West.
Why, Wadsworth was a wheatfield! Once we bought
(Five dollars down and five a month) two building lots
On Wadsworth south of Alameda. It's The Villa now.
(We stopped our five-a-month and let it go!)
Does anyone but me recall the sign on Broadway South
The horse with wings, high flying horse?
Some gasoline or other message there.
'Twas gasoline and cars that brought him down, of course.
And killed the street cars, paved the highways,
Filled up all those wheatfields,
Put an end to Denver Dry, Montaldo's,
D. and F. and all the rest.
Progress it's called. But me,
I'd like my Denver back.

OLD FARMER'S WIFE REMEMBERS

The city screams outside my window!
Strangers I will never know
Stand by my side in super-markets;
Sit on left and right in buses
And at worship. Many years have passed
Since children played in summer fields;
Rode horses through green pastures;
Felt the quiet Spring unfold
Its blossoms; gathered 'round
An Autumn bonfire, or gladly watched
The snowdrifts close the roads,
Close out the world.

Time in its inexorable process
Paved the pastures;
Changed children into adults;
Animals, well loved, live
Only in my memory.
The city screams outside my window!
My world is filled with strangers
I will never know.

Written 1987 – 1988

Jake on Main Street, Sabetha, 1950s.

LAURA

Laura who is not much more than five
Has learned that numbers build upon themselves
And go from ten to—thousands, all by themselves
They do not stop, unless they want to.

Laura, who is not much more than five
Thinks of growing old, and dying.
People are like numbers. They get old all by themselves.
They do not stop, even if they want to.

Laura, who is not much more than five
Thinks it would be better if people
Found the number that is last of all the numbers
Then would stick there! (Do we want to?)

Written in 1989

*Laura Bethany Lefkow, on "her rock"
in Yosemite, 1989.*

OLD WOMAN

I am a house abandoned.
Haunted by inhabitants of my past
Long gone. Weathered by time,
I stand alone
Unused, unloved, unneeded,
Wearing with what dignity remains
Some remnants of a time
When, if not grace, at least, utility
Was mine.

I wait the Wrecker's ball
When with a sigh
I fall and leave a space
For building.

As published in New Zealandia, *1996*

CURTAIN'S FALL

I am old. The mirror and the calendar
Agree. The solemn facts are these:
The curtain soon will fall;
My role on this small stage
Will be played out and I shall lie
In Woodlawn's quiet graveyard
Where a stone will tell my name
To those who pass—
And that, is that!

Or, is it?
There are hints of mysteries:
Flowers grow from bulbs and seeds so dead
(As dead as I shall be) and butterflies emerge
From "graves" as dark as mine!
And there is in my heart a sense of timelessness
As though this "resident within"
Was never made for Time;
The spirit of the child, adult and aged
Is the same; my fading eyes look with surprise
Upon the image in the glass.

And then, the only One who knows for sure
Has said, "Don't let your heart be troubled…"
So, I wait and with sometimes fragile faith
Prepare as best I can for this,
Life's last adventure. This life
(That never was my own but came
By other will than mine) will pass.
What mystery!

Written between 1988 and 2004

SONG OF AN OLD FARMHOUSE

I am a house where children are,
Not one, nor two or three, but four!
Not model children in any way
But normal kids who work and play
Inside my somewhat battered door.
When company comes they often see
A distraught mistress and an upset me
For lions lurk under upturned chairs
Superman in a bath towel flies my stairs
And the general confusion is something to see!
But even if I'm neat I wear
A slightly distracted and self-conscious air.
If my surfaces shine, unaccustomedly glowing
I've an uneasy feeling my scratches are showing!
So, if unexpected, you knock on my door
When the rugs are awry and the books on the floor,
Please ignore my condition; come on in and see
The uninhibited family who live in me.

Written in the 1940s

Joan, John, Tom, and
Judy Humphrey, 1947.

I SPEAK OF SIMPLE THINGS

LINES TO A CHRISTMAS TREE

Down you come! Off with the bright bedizenment
And lights. It's time to go!
Oh, yes, I know
The holidays are barely over and the snow
Lies deep upon the lawn.
You're lovely still, only a little dry.
Can anyone tell why
A tree should come inside
And being hung with nonsense things,
Acquire a sudden magic all its own?
Why, dazzled by your glow, the whole world stops,
The tone of living changes,
For a time, Love reigns, Joy fills the heart,
We bow before a King we scarcely know—
But, oh! It's such a foolish magic, people say,
And you have had your day.
The festive time has gone and life goes on,
It's time we stopped pretending to be gay!

Written between 1964 and 1975

THIRTEEN-NINETY-FIVE

There you are;
Quiet, lonely on your corner;
Your "For Sale" sign so neatly placed
And all the busy clutter of our habitation
Gone.

Why do I feel this pain
As though your loneliness were also mine?
We did not like each other much
Through all the years together, you and I;
I was too much for you. Arrogant in your youth
You made my old possessions look anachronistic
And consistently refused to make them welcome.

And remember how it was with guests? They'd say,
"Oh, what a pretty house!" and you'd be smug;
But I would have to find a place to put them—
You wouldn't give an inch!

I have to say it to be honest.
My new-old house is better,
Fits my age and near-antiques and seems
Completely to cooperate.

Why is it then,
This hurting, tearing feeling of abandonment?
You will be loved and more than likely
Quite appreciated;
And soon I'll come to feel "at home" again.
All this is better for us both.
Goodbye, dear house, dear home,
Goodbye.

Written circa 1975

*Tom and John Humphrey inside the barn on the
farm where Donna and Jake reared their
children, as it appeared in 2005.*

*Coloma feeding the chickens at a farm
south of Woodlawn, Kansas, 1940s.*

LEAVETAKING

Goodbye, old home, old farm.
Goodbye to elm trees, wind-battered, brave,
Cloaking nakedness each Spring
With gallant greenery. Your branches held our swings
And sheltered shyest dreams doomed to impossibility.

Goodbye, green fields and walnut grove
And willow trees down by the spring
Where fresh, sweet water bubbled up, unfailing.

Goodbye to coming home, welcomed as we topped the rise
Of hill by red-roofed house and weathered barns
That wore their age in silver-gray
Whose sagging beams and smooth-worn mangers
Spoke of animals long gone but well remembered.

We sold a farm: A reasonable transaction;
Signed our names on legal papers here and there
And walked away. It was quite simple at the outset
We held a piece of paper in our hands
Representing money, turned and walked away.

We have a bit of time to put it all together
"Possession to be given on a certain day."
How can I leave—in May, when all this world
Is fresh and sweet? But, in October, how?
For then the air is crisp, the leaves are gold and bronze
And apple orchards drop their windfall fruit.

Oh, I am caught in the immutability of decision made
And certainty that something of my life
Will somehow stay, singing itself out.
In wind-swept grass and falling leaves.
I will go. I'll go and not return!
I'll go, but oh, my heart will stay!

Written in 1960

DAWN

Dawn is singing
    sweet and high
Her instrument
    is a drawn curtain
    muting full intensity
Her mighty chorus
    has a guest soloist today
    a butterfly
        on the pane
            behind the curtain
        maybe fresh from cocoon
            waving wings of dawn
            making all ready
                for this day's journey

Dawn is singing
    sweet and high
Themes of faith
    quiet and subtle
    proven true once again
Hope in sunlight
    baking away cold dew
        that sleep distributed
        upon the grounds
            of my heart
Lovingly warming
    the walls
        of my tiny house

Written between 1987 and 1988

WANDERLUST

I have a love affair with places;
All countrysides, all cities, small and great.
Milwaukee's old Germanic houses, fortress-like
They are; I want to see inside! I want to stay!
And there's Chicago's gritty Loop, the El,
Marshall Fields, Lincoln Park, the Art Museum
And the Lake-front; white-sailed boats in summer.
I see me in a Lake Shore flat! I want to stay!
But then there is Puget Sound; the lovely San Juan Islands;
And Seattle! Nordic, fog-draped, America's Queen City,
Seattle! I want to live in that blue house, up high—there!
On that hill! But then, there's San Francisco, and Carmel!
There's no place I should live except Carmel!—except, perhaps,
In Kona! Captain Cook and Kailua! The sea is really aqua in Hawaii!
There are sandy beaches, white and black in Kona, and those sunsets
On the ocean! I'd love a house up on a mountain—there!
I see me in a wicker chair on the lanai with sea and sky and
Bougainvillea!

But then there's Kansas! I grew up in Kansas!
Black plowed fields in Springtime, miles of meadows,
Wheat fields deeply gold in summer; apple orchards,
Trees all red and golden in the autumn; all my past
Calls me to come and stay! But this I know:
One life is much too short. The siren songs of other places
Are just fantasy. There's this little house
Close to the towering Rockies. This is home!

I WILL FORGET

I will not dream again;
The years I spent forgetting
Can't be wasted, vain.
My heart has built new life around the scar
As pearls are formed to heal a wounded
Mollusk's pain.
I will not think again
Of how your arms around me
Tumbled all my poor defenses down;
Rather, I'll re-live
Those bleak, gray days when you were gone;
I've set a guard around my heart.
My dreams shall be for those who share my days
I'll keep the longing buried deeper yet
And, help me, kindly time,
I will forget.

MEMORY

I must have loved him.
I still can feel
The texture of his coat
Against my face.
It was goodbye and well it was goodbye
And the remembered pain is just
The faintest shadow on my heart.
But though I recall with clarity
The rough wool of his coat,
The color, even, and the tears
I can't recall his face!

OCTOBER SONG

The chilling winds came early on
Stilling for all time, I thought,
The April tumult. Long before September
I had made my peace with Autumn,
Winter held no menace, there is peace
In frozen stillness.
Then you came, by chance, unbidden;
Came and went, and did not go,
And would not go, and so
I placed you on a high shelf of my mind
Pretending you were gone;
But from your hiding place
A quiet, warming presence
Brought an ill-timed renascence of Spring.
Winter still will come, and soon,
But broken is my truce with Autumn.

Written between 1988 and 2004

ANECDOTE

They both recalled the summer day
Across the years and miles that lay between them:
She drove along a country road
And through a meadow, wild and sweet.
The sun-swept fragrance of the grass, wind-borne,
Exhumed the buried longings in a breath of time
And they emerged, full strength, with near forgotten power
To twist and tear the heart. She shivered
And the man beside her smiled and asked, mundanely,
"See a ghost?" She turned her tear-blurred eyes away
And answered, "No, not really."

He sat at luncheon with a friend
And talked of business and the like.
When by his table walked a girl
Who wore a perfume, meadow-sweet. He lost
His train of thought mid-sentence. Absently
He turned his glass around—and 'round
And then, returning to the present moment
And the friend, and with a reminiscent grin
Remarked, "Have I told you about this girl I knew?"

Written between 1964 and 1975

SO LONG AGO

So long ago
In agony of heart
I thought I heard You say,
"I have seen his ways
And will heal him!"

Was it Your voice
Or only what I wished to hear?
I marked it, wrote the date.
And year by year
Remember.

And wait.

WIDOW'S SONG

Like the falling rain
On the thirsting field
Softly as a dream
Or the sound of tears
Comes your voice to me
Through the mist of years
Silent in my heart
Silent to my ears.

Walk, my love, with me
Though my steps are slow
You've gone on before
Teach me how to go.
Wait, my love, for me
By the open door
May we be again
As we were before.

Jake and Donna on their wedding day,
October 6, 1933.

Willis on tricycle.

COUSINS
For R.M.S.

They made a place together all that summer;
The girl, exiled to Grandma's house and homesick
And the boy exiled from childhood
By an illness-with-no-answer. They were ten
That summer, cousins sharing loneliness and pain.
She kindly made herself content to play
The quiet games of "let's pretend" his strength allowed.
Patiently she climbed into the ancient buggy
Sitting staid beside him as he drove his team to town.
They shared the treats his mother made
And secrets. She, the hopeless homesick tears
She shed alone, avoiding Gran's displeasure;
He, how tired he was of being sick. He told
Of days when he, too sick to play, would sleep,
And of a dream he had of playgrounds
Cool and green, of playing there like other kids.
Then the question he could ask no other,
"Will I die, you think? Am I going to die?"
"Of course not! Kids don't die,
You're just a kid!" she said, and reassured,
He smiled and urged his horses on their way.
Summer ended. She went home to family and school,
Her exile done. He, one dark November night
Went on to find the green and happy playground
Of his dream.

About Donna's brother,
Willis Owen Glenn (1919–1930),
and their cousin, Rovena Glenn Smith

John holding Tom; Joan and Judy, 1945.

*Joan; John with wife, Janice, and son, Brian;
Jake, Donna, Tom; Judy and husband, Rex, 1960.*

HEART'S GARDEN

Joan is like a wild rose;
Judy is a daisy;
Tommy is a buttercup;
    Round and fat and lazy;
John grows like a tall young tree,
    With only sky to bound it
Within the garden of my heart,
    With walls of love around it.

Written in 1945
Published in The Poetry Forum, *June 22, 1958*

SEQUEL, 1960

"Daisy" soon is being married,
"Wild Rose" is a pert brunette.
 To my tall young freshman, Tommy,
"Buttercup's" an epithet!
 John, my tree, has been transplanted
Far away, with wife and son,
 While I, in my deserted garden
Wonder where the years have gone.

"Heart's Garden" and "Sequel" were published together
in The Denver Post, *February 7, 1960*

TO MY CHILDREN

I do not wish my love to be to you a chain
Though forged of earth's most precious substance
For a chain would bind, restrain, and in the end,
Enslave you. Rather I would wish my love to be
A silver thread of music reaching out
Across unmeasured time and space, unheard,
Until some need of yours, some memory, perhaps,
Shall prompt your hearts to tune it in, and then,
That it shall be a symphony complete
To cheer or comfort or sustain.

I do not wish my faith to be to you a wall.
A wall declares, "So far, no farther may you go!"
Instead, I wish that this faith I hold dear
Shall be your door—wide open—
To the deeper, richer secrets of the soul.
That as my body gave you entrance into mortal life,
This travail of my spirit, bent in prayer,
Should bring you to the second birth
That gives the first its meaning,
Robs the grave of grief and takes from life
The tragic frenzy and despair.

I do not wish your lives to be a trophy I may show;
Status symbol of parenthood, in whose reflected glow
I warm myself. My hopes for you are these:
Self-realization, self-acceptance, and gratitude,
That, being given much, you will do what you can.
I wish you love; someone with whom to share
Your walk and quiet talk. Some satisfying work,
That, being done, will leave the sad world
Just a bit less sad. And for myself, just this:
Remember me with kindness. Take from me
The false halo of Motherhood! Regard me
As a woman only. Faulty, stumbling, unsure;
Loving, oftentimes unwisely—Oh, but well!
Remember me with kindness.
I will be content.

As published in Church and Home, *September 1968*

Donna with John, Judy, Michael Lefkow, Joan,
Tom and Pat, September 2000, on the occasion
of Joan's induction as a federal judge.

VISIT AT A REST HOME

The work-worn hands lay idle in her lap.
From time to time she took a bit of fabric of her skirt
And smoothed it in a pleat. The room is large and shabby.
From a corner comes the Indianapolis race in loud and living color.
Her tone is soft and gentle as she speaks
Of these about, who share her present days, these strangers,
Vacant-faced, some young, some old, all derelict,
The offal of our lives whose lives are past
Or never were. Blessedly,
She thought she came but yesterday
And may be off tomorrow. "I have to go,
You know, I just do what they say," she smiled.
She thought it must be suppertime. "I've not a thing
Prepared," she said, in soft apology. "I wish you could
Have a meal with us." We murmured that we'd eaten,
And remembered those good times
When we'd all gathered 'round her table, snowy spread,
To eat the bounty of her useful days; the home-baked bread,
The garden beans, and home-cured ham. We asked
If those who care for her are kind. "Oh, yes," she said.
"I don't need babying, you know."

I glanced up at my daughter, standing tall beside her
Face awash with tears, although her smile was brave and bright.
(The men with empty eyes stared boldly, bleakly
At her slim, young legs.) At last, I said
That we must go. "I wish that you could stay, and then
I'd have someone to visit with 'til bedtime."
Then, as though she'd been too selfish, "But, I know,
Your time is short. That coat is light. Take care
You don't get cold! (It's May, outside, with flowers everywhere.)
Have a good trip, and let me know when you get home."
We left. And clung together weeping in the soft May dusk.
Did we cry for that frail, patient lady in the shabby chair,
For our dear, shared past, or for ourselves?
We do not know.

Written in 1971, after a visit with Jake's mother, Bertie Humphrey

JONI

Just an
Ordinary little girl, really,
Nothing unusual at all.
In fact, to prove it, I'll
Define her!

A Mona Lisa smile in a pixie face,
Wide eyes and dark
Straight hair, prediction
Of a loveliness to be, and in her hands
Nothing at all.
Excepting just our hearts!

Written for Joni Dawson Aue,
Patricia Dawson Humphrey's sister,
between 1962 and 1963

Joan and Judy on a boat ride,
Kansas Free Fair, Topeka, 1950.

I SPEAK OF SIMPLE THINGS

A DAY AT THE FAIR

My mother died that summer.
"After a long illness," in September
My mother died. I left her room
And hurried home to change. I took time out
To make a cake to please the children
And after all those days and nights
When I returned, "She's gone!" they said.

The family came home, friends gathered in,
And then the funeral. I did the proper thing
And said appropriate words
And felt nothing at all.

The next day was the last day of the Fair.
My kids had missed a lot that summer
So I said, "Tomorrow, let's go to the Fair!"
My husband smiled, "O.K., you guys,
Up early now!" and all four scurried
Happily to bed.

Late that September afternoon I sat alone
Waiting for the last ride to be over
The old fairground was filled with people,
There was noise and laughter, hucksters
Pled their cause, the raucous carousel,
The dust and heat. I sat alone and waited.

Suddenly, in all that noise
And with no shred of warning
The ice-jam in my heart gave way.
Dry-eyed and silent came my last
Good-bye.

As published in New Zealandia, *November 1992*
About Coloma's death on September 11, 1950

WISH

I do not wish you
Joy without sorrow
Nor endless day
Without the healing dark
Nor brilliant sun
Without the restful shadow
Nor tides that never turn
Against your bark.
I wish you love
And strength and faith
And wisdom, good enough
To help some needy one.
I wish you songs, but also
Blessed silence…and God's
Sweet peace, when every day is done.

Written in 1974

JOAN

I have never tried to set down my feelings about you.
Perhaps it is because the feelings I have
Run too deep for words.
Also my feeling is inadequacy
When I try for words to tell you of my thoughts;
For you are the one who always seems to tear away
The shabby, artificial wrappings of my sentences, to leave me
With the small, and often meaningless kernel of my thoughts
Wondering why I thought that what I had to say
Was of the slightest moment. Now tonight,
With what I call my "heart" so full of pain and love—
If I know love—if I must say it badly,
Then it will be badly said.
The tearing, hurting, loving battle has to end.
The time for "Mother"
Long has gone. Now, let me be your friend.

Joan, 1968.

PATRICIA

Petite, dark-eyed, and faintly oriental in
Appearance. (Maybe some forgotten forebear
Traveled briefly in Japan and took a bride!)
"Ruth" in skinny pants and sweatshirt, to whom
If timing had been right, I might have been "Naomi."
Casually she danced into our world—and out—and left
It with an empty space shaped
Almost like a daughter.

Written in 1964
Patricia and Thomas Humphrey
were married April 21, 1966

Patricia Elizabeth Dawson,
1964.

TO TOMMY, AGED 19

The Youngest, who could never bear to be the Youngest!
Hurry to grow—hurry to have—hurry to be!
Only then to wait the catching up of many
Passed along the way in all your rush.
As stormy as a Kansas thunderhead
Spilling its fury briefly, then, released,
Glinting with sunlight, caught by summer wind
Lifted and out of sight—so, your quicksilver
Ever-changing moods. Self-distrusting—
Needing much to win, but winning
Never quite enough.

Have you considered, as you chafe
Under the weight of circumstance
Made not by but for you—
Pressed intolerably into a mold
Hewed out for other forms than yours, that
Reason for your being You—uniquely?
Enter now into the search for self-hood with all
Youthful abandon, and finding Self, be satisfied.

Written in 1965

Thomas Glenn Humphrey,
1962.

63

FOR A DAUGHTER LEAVING

She's leaving, Lord.
All that we said, all that we did,
All that we were just made her want the more
To go.
Tonight I read the words You said
So long ago. "My soul is filled with sorrow
Unto death." I, tonight,
Feel sorrow, unto death.
But You said, "not my will but Yours…"
And I, unwilling, I must say it too.
Since there's no choice.

Go with her, Lord!
Dispatch some angel just to guard her way!
Give to her troubled spirit some real sense
Of Your unchanging love.
Be in her mind for quietness and peace
And do not let her stray one step
Beyond Your caring. Teach her wisdom, Lord.
Deal gently with her weakness and her need
And in Your time, oh, bring her home again.

Written in 1971

Rex, Glen, Joel and Judy Kauffman, 1971.

TO ANNE WHO IS EIGHT

If I should go to find a little girl
To have and hold for all the years there are
Then there should be some guidelines, firmly set,
Not subject to debate or compromise.
She should be just *so* tall, with wide blue eyes
Or maybe gray (sometimes it's hard to tell),
But fringed with lashes down to *here*! That long!
She should have hair like cornsilk, sugar spun
That softly curls and tangles in the wind;
A princess on vacation from her princess-ing
With smudgy cheeks and scrapey knees from playing;
A girl-child, something like—a marigold, perhaps?
And having found her, I would call her
Anne.

Written in 1970

Anne Leslie Humphrey, 1972.

TO LAURIE WITH LOVE
AND DISAGREEMENT

Let me tell you, Laurie, dear
About your friend, the mouse.
When I was just about your age
Those pests ate up my house!

They chewed away the plaster
Ate holes beneath the doors
They ate the food off of the shelves
And skittered on the floors.

They made their nests, those mother-mice
In every nook and cranny
In backs of closets, in our shoes,
You never saw so many!

They crawled in the piano
And made their little nests
They fixed it so it wouldn't play
The vicious little pests!

And so, my friend, I must insist
No "ifs" no "ands" no "buts"
Though you may think that mice are nice
I hate their little guts!

Written in 1981 or 1982

Laurel Elizabeth Humphrey, 1980.

LAURA

My heart was taken early
By a child of miniature proportions.
Tall for three, she was, and slim, blue-eyed
And lovely. Home from pre-school she appeared
At noon upon my doorstep. There was a code:
She'd say, "I'm hungry!" "What would you like today?"
I'd say. "Guess!" she'd say, and I would think,
And think, and then—"Cottage cheese!
An egg. And applesauce?" "Okay," she'd say
And then with sparkling eyes, "What else?"
On cue I'd say, "Well, what about some cold hot-chocolate!"
She knew I'd guess it; we played it every day.

She's older now. She'll soon be six.
I'm far away; we see each other now and then.
My heart was taken early by a child called
Laura.

Written in 1990

*Laura Bethany Lefkow
in Grandma Donna's rocker, 1987–88.*

FROM DREAMS, REALITY

The Real is but the dream
Brought to fruition.
We hold a thing of beauty
In our hands: Reality—
But it began in Someone's mind.
A dream that, nourished,
Grew to bring delight.

A dream is fragile and its light
Will fail without the faith
That fans the embers.

Trust your dreams;
One dream made real can light
Your life and make it glow
Through all your years.

*Written for Carol Peitzmeier
on her retirement in 1987*

FOR ELSA

The dark mystery
That we call Death
Has overtaken and has borne away
This one who has been
Our familiar friend.

Although in all our life
We are in death,
We still believe
That in You, in our death
We are in Life!

And so, we pray
That through the way marked "Exit"
From our sight
This one whom we have loved
Has found the door wide-open
To the world of light
And that she has heard
Your voice say, "Welcome home!"

Written for Elsa Kennedy

THE PASTOR'S WIFE
SAYS GOODBYE

When I was very young
I fell in love with life.
With fun, adventure, learning,
Friends—all that natural life and youth
Presented I explored. And then,
I fell in love with God!
And life took on new meaning. Peace,
A settled joy, a sense of inner happiness
I had not known before were mine.

And then I came to love a man
And with him, came to live among you.
You took me to your hearts,
So now, my love for God, this man
And you, my friends, is so entwined
That I can barely separate the three.

You are my family in my heart;
Your children, mine, your happiness or pain,
My own, and mine is yours,
So closely have our lives been joined
Through all these years together.

But Time's inexorable process
Brings a closure. My role among you
Changes though my love remains unchanged.
Since God in love
Has knit our lives together, may He now
In this new circumstance
Still keep us one.

Written for Blanche H. Davis, 1990

THE WIDOWS

We are everywhere
We with our perms
Our little purses,
Our careful steps
Supported by our walkers
Or our canes.
We are the survivors.
Years ago we laid our men away
And though
We did not know it then
Our own significance
As well.

We're all about you;
In the churches, in the shops:
We lunch; we bide our time.
People smile, indulging us,
They hold the doors
We thank them, grateful
(Truly. Doors are heavy!)
We wait. We are polite and quiet
("Don't make a fuss!")
We're the survivors.

Bertie Humphrey, Jake's mother, with
Donna in Jake and Donna's home in
Sabetha, about 1962.

MAN IN HIS WISDOM

Man, searching for transcendency while rejecting
The One to whom his fathers bent the knee
Finds many things to worship. A god of stone
Is hardly less a god than all these bright possessions;
But worshipers of idols in their day
Were comforted in ignorance by the faith
With which they practiced their obeisance.
Man, now so wise, knows this will never do
So he must make his own—each in his likeness—
Out of wisdom of his mind he makes a god,
Controlled, convenient and predictable;
Comforting, when comfort of a sort is needed;
Never troubling or incomprehensible. It is written,
Is it not, "In the image of Man created He Him"?

Written between 1964 and 1975

THE KENNEDYS

Stern and angry in their grief
They stand before our million eyes
They walk, heads up, with level gaze
Unbending. Their children walk in strength
Dry-eyed and grimly proud.

Tall, strong, and unyielding in the glaring lights
They go. Letting the heart break
But not the spirit. Humbly, they bow,
Meekly they kneel, but only to their God.

Written in November 1963

THE BIGOT WITH THE BOOK

Behold, you, there! The servant of the Lord!
I come to speak for Jesus; He is mine;
He walks and talks with me and opens doors
That you may hear me speak. So, Hear!
The Book is in my hand to give
Authority to the bitter, fear-filled words
I hurl upon you, setting man against another,
Race against race. In ignorance and fear
I use the holy fire to set aflame
A holocaust of hate, and, satisfied
I stand and watch it burn.

Written between 1964 and 1975

TODAY IN A QUIET CHURCH

Today in a quiet church
From the hand of a business-suited gentleman
I accepted a bit of bread
And a tiny cup of wine
"In remembrance of Me!"
What is there in this small ritual
That is relevant to the lives
Of middle-class Americans of the twentieth—
The dying twentieth—century?
To remember a grave, young God
Breaking a loaf, and saying,
"This is My body!" And the cup,
"This is My blood!"
Not relevant, you say. Oh, no?
Then why do we sit quiet in a way
Much more than worship-quiet.
We are still. Our heads are bowed.
Holding the cup, the wine beats with the beat
Of our heart's blood, trembles in our hands.
Drink ye, all of it…it trickles down our throats;
Surreptitiously we brush away a tear
And do not meet our neighbors' eyes
As we depart.

The Woodlawn Baptist Church
where the Glenn and Humphrey
families worshipped.

75

CHRISTMAS...AGAIN!

I could not hear the angels sing
(The carols were so loud)
Nor was there much good will in me
As I pushed through the crowd
Of Christmas shoppers in the stores
Deciding what to buy;
The time is short, the pressure's on
Somehow I've to try
To make a place for Christmas
In this madness. Where to start?
Not here, I thought, I'm going home
There's nothing in my heart
That speaks of Christmas!

I walked into my quiet house;
I brewed a cup of tea;
And settled in a chair alone
To think. How can it be
That all that's left of Christmas
Is this manic need to buy?
But giving is a grace, I thought,
For others! This is why
We crowd the stores at Christmas time
Selecting this and that;
To show our love? If this is so,
Then why this flat
Depression?

I read the story once again
To hear it in my heart!
The Prophet ecstasies, the Star,
The Magi! That's the part
I love the most; those Eastern potentates
Who somehow knew a King was born
And left their proud estates
To find Him. Now, although
The centuries have passed,
The story's told year after year
And even through the vast
Cacophony of nonsense there's a still,
Mysterious power
That drives a world that's lost its way
To celebrate this hour.
This "Christ-Mass!"

So, on with Christmas! Ring those bells!
It's still the world's best hope!
For Christ is born! The Story's true!
Drag out the tinsel rope,
Bedeck the halls, hang mistletoe!
And let the candles glow!
Bring out the crèche, the holly wreath!
It's lunacy, I know…
The lovely lunacy of Christmas!

Written in 1990
Published in New Zealandia, *December 1991*

BETH

I wasn't really looking when I found you
But you were there (not that you were waiting!
Both of us had sort of put "the quest" aside).
But you were there! There must have been a plan
For you were Kansas! I was Texas!
What odds that we should meet and fall in love!

And so we called our people in and had a wedding!
You were lovely in that gorgeous dress!
All the folks who loved us gathered 'round
And we were married! And I thought I really loved you!

Since that day we've shared great times, hard times,
Success and un-success and changing homes
And jobs (and diapers), gains and losses
And I need to tell you that I really love you!
Wife and lover, mother of my children
Steady, wise and sacrificial in your giving;
Funny, Generous, Beloved,
Beth.

Written at Sto Stevens' request as an anniversary gift
to his wife Beth (Jake's niece) in 2001

PALM SUNDAY LATE AT NIGHT

The concert ended; we had heard
The symphony and chorus
In the auditorium
Proclaim the Easter message.
With Handel's "Hallelujah"
Ringing in our ears.
We poured out to the cool Spring night
And there, higher, on a staircase,
A man proclaimed with all his might:
"Repent! Believe! Christ is the Way!"
His words near lost in sound of happy voices
Heading for the parking lot.

My two companions shook their heads,
Agreeing in distaste, "These zealots!
Shouting their religion! These people
Seem to come from everywhere,
This wild, offensive ranting
Is a gross intrusion."

I thought of John, the Baptist,
Hurling prophecies and warnings,
Dressed in skins, unshaven,
Wilderness-bred.

I said nothing.

BONDAGE

I am in bondage, Lord.
Enslaved.
Habit chains me to the repetition of the same old sins.
The pride
That finds it not a thing incredible
This cosmic stooping to my need
For joy. That You should bend
And send
Your spirit, drenched in love
For my unlove. And yet
That I in pride withhold to bend
And send
My love to heal my brother's hurt.

Oh come, Oh come, Immanuel, Come!
Strike off this chain and set this captive free
To honor Thee with love returned
Who has since life began, loved only self.
Give me at this late day, Your power
To grow and give, Oh, my God, to love.

GRACE

"…And the wise ones and those of understanding will say, "Why do you receive these men?' And the Christ replies, 'This is why I receive them, O ye of understanding, that not one of them believed himself worthy of this.' And he will hold out his hands to us and we shall fall down before Him…and we shall weep…and we shall understand all things!…Lord, thy kingdom come!"

Dostoyevsky, Crime and Punishment, *Part I, Chapter II (1917)*

Someone said that if we'd run our race with patience;
Fought the good fight, then that which lies ahead
Shall hold no dread. My years grow short; soon
I shall cross that river. Sometimes my faith
Is fragile. Does His grace suffice
For races badly run and lost;
For battles sadly fought, the whole war, even?
I falter, then remember that it was for sinners,
Failures such as I You died; I think of this
And sometimes there's a glint of iridescent joy
And wonder that by grace amazing You await
Your ragged, beaten stragglers; these
Losers in a race too long.

HOPE

It seemed the night would never end;
We've fallen in the ditches
Dragging with us our companions
Struggling out, we've ground their faces
In the mud.

There's been no sign from You
That we could read, but then
We have no common speech
Or shared tradition.

Some seem to hear You say,
"This is the way, or that."
But now, at least we know
That we are lost;
As men who stumble in the dark
In unfamiliar lands; we know
That left to our own way, this night
Will never end.

Give us a Key; a Word whereby
We may translate the signs and symbols.
Turn our babel tongues to sanity!
There is a Star! And does the Eastern sky
Begin to glow with light?

As published in New Zealandia, *1995*

KING'S X

I am a Christian. I believe
That Jesus is God's Son and that He died
And rose again, and that it was for me.
This is my faith, such as it is
And in this faith is all the hope I have.
But in the office where I work
Are men and women, who
Have never known this Way at all;
And there I am; I speak no word
For I am there, you see—
I who am filled with envy
Self-conceit and ridicule.
I see the need they have and, God,
I dare not say a word, though I know well
How You have said, "Go, ye…"
I fear that I am one who bears Your name
And keeps her fingers crossed.

Published in Christianity Today, *March 4, 1966*
Re-titled "Exempt?" by the magazine

LIGHT

You came to light all men
And surely it is true
That where light shines at all
That light is You.
And yet — and yet —
The darkness is so deep!
Pain, hunger, war, the stench of Hell
Pervades the world, perverts the minds of men
So they call evil good
And use the little light they have
To show the way to deeper darkness still.
Oh, Dayspring, haste the day
When You shall rise for all men, everywhere.
When in Your blazing Presence
We at last shall see.
When the foul, fetid darkness shall be burned away
And men shall know that You are Light
And follow and be free.

MAUNDY THURSDAY

Solemnly in unaccustomed candlelight
The people wait. There is no whispered word;
Shoulder to shoulder, yet alone
Each worshiper sits quietly,
Self before Self, and each must hear
The silent accusation of his heart.

Christ Jesus, are You really here, unseen
Behind this little table as I go
To take the cup and wafer, make my prayer,

Then take again my place while others come?
This hour set parenthetic to a busy week
Is hardly time enough to search the soul
For hidden sin. This mind, so full
Of balance sheets (and bombs!)
Cost records and the like,
Finds this return to Calvary too far!
Confused I stand before the real
And Extra-real.

Lord, is there sustenance here—for me—
Or, shall I be forevermore unfed?

Published in Christianity Today, *March 26, 1965*

PETITION

My thoughts turn ragged
When I try to pray
Falling in pieces, flying about
Settling here and there
But never where I need to bring them—
To Your throne.
And so, with pen in hand
I catch them, pin them down
And hold them fast to paper.

Hear, my Lord, these words I write;
As thoughts flow through my pen
I sense my lostness. The words
Controlled and circumspect
Bear small relation to the turmoil
In my heart.

Could I but see You at my door
Waiting for admittance?
Are You truly there? There are
So many barriers to my soul
That only Grace can shatter.
Where's the key? This door is firmly fast,
The locks are old and rusted. Lord,
Please break and enter
Or I die.

PRAYER

Not only for our overt sins
But for our praying, Lord, Thy mercy!

"We thank Thee for our daily bread," we murmur,
Casually, "Bless to our body's need, we pray. Amen."
And so partake
Of that which in another day
Had been a king's repast—and do not care
That not "our body's need" but often greed
Is this we call on Thee to bless.
While Hunger stalks the world
And millions die in bleak despair?
Forgive us Lord, our little daily prayer.

"Oh, Lord, my child now brings to birth
Her first-born! Be Thou near
To give her doctors wisdom, skill—
Keep child and mother safe in Thy protecting care.
Amen." While on a filthy street, somewhere
A child is born. The street-louts watch
And mock the woman's pain and curse the offspring
In the slough of blood. (Thy mercy on Thy people, Lord!)
Our baby sleeps soft as a child of royal birth.
The street-child dies—or what is worse
He lives, to die another day.
"Thou God of all the earth, forgive me these
Near blasphemies," I whisper—on my knees!

Written in 1963

PRAYER OF AN OFFICE WORKER

Go with me, Lord, as I approach the city
Cloaked in morning mists that the now-rising sun
Will soon dispel. Here, Lord, the giant, merchandise,
Is king, and we who crowd the freeways day by day
Are his obedient servants.
Be in my mind no still, small voice today
Or I will never hear You speak at all
Above the roar of commerce and my own
Self-seeking voice within.
Speak strong within my heart.
Shout down the thoughtless word
And let me see the hurting needs around me.
Let me gently speak a healing word.

Published in New Zealandia, *July 1993*

Donna in November 1981.
Denver skyline is in the background.

THOUGHTS WHILE IN CHURCH

Not for this was the Race invaded
The arms stretched out and the Life given!
Not for this! This "Church somnolent"
Restively waiting the benediction.

Visit again, O God, Thy people!
Kindle among us the cleansing fire!
Burn out the pious pretenses and make us
Able to worship Thee, God, as Thou art!

Published in Christianity Today, *March 12, 1963*

THE WAY

Today and tomorrow and yesterday, I am both and neither.
Today, I told You that, in all my lack of love for You,
I still must know You. I said that I would trust You with the civil war
That is my life. How long I can maintain this trust I do not know,
But You said, "You will not believe unless you see
Some signs and wonders." That is what I want to see.
And then I saw a glimmer of some hunger for Your help
In one of my young, loved ones. She's been a long way off
And yet, a hunger and a glow of promise certainly was there.
I'll take it as an evidence that You are here and working
In our alienation. Let me go from here to some new faith myself
And as I take my bed and walk, make a trail of some sort
That will help her and the others know there is a way.

In this I trust You. In my unbelief and emptiness of heart
I still believe. The way I go from here I do not know.
There will be failure, agony of mind and soul. Deep doubt
That I am in Your plan and love at all will still assail.
But this day I, at least, can say, I want to live
And move and have my being in Your plan and purpose.
One step, and then another. And the next. I think I'd better burn this bed!
Good-by, you pool where doubtful angels stir the waters,
I think I'm on my way.

Written in Summer, 1972

Donna in Denver,
early 1990s.

*The following pages record Donna's genealogy
from 1799 to 2007, along with photos
of her descendants as of March 2005.*

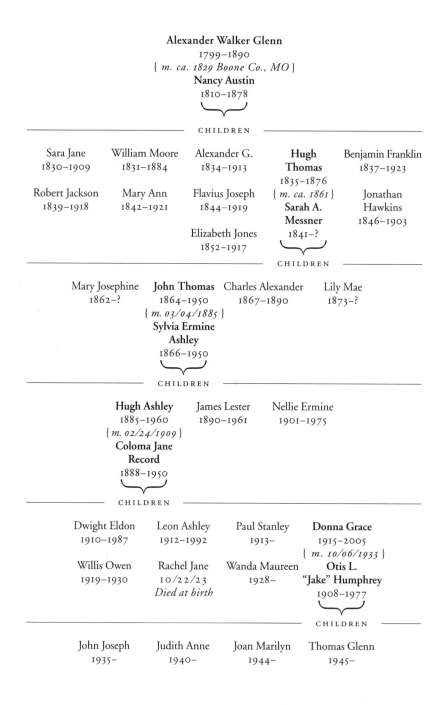

Alexander Walker Glenn
1799–1890
{ *m. ca. 1829 Boone Co., MO* }
Nancy Austin
1810–1878

CHILDREN

Sara Jane	William Moore	Alexander G.	**Hugh**	Benjamin Franklin
1830–1909	1831–1884	1834–1913	**Thomas**	1837–1923
			1835–1876	
Robert Jackson	Mary Ann	Flavius Joseph	{ *m. ca. 1861* }	Jonathan
1839–1918	1842–1921	1844–1919	**Sarah A.**	Hawkins
			Messner	1846–1903
		Elizabeth Jones	1841–?	
		1852–1917		

CHILDREN

Mary Josephine	**John Thomas**	Charles Alexander	Lily Mae
1862–?	1864–1950	1867–1890	1873–?
	{ *m. 03/04/1885* }		
	Sylvia Ermine		
	Ashley		
	1866–1950		

CHILDREN

Hugh Ashley	James Lester	Nellie Ermine
1885–1960	1890–1961	1901–1975
{ *m. 02/24/1909* }		
Coloma Jane		
Record		
1888–1950		

CHILDREN

Dwight Eldon	Leon Ashley	Paul Stanley	**Donna Grace**
1910–1987	1912–1992	1913–	1915–2005
			{ *m. 10/06/1933* }
Willis Owen	Rachel Jane	Wanda Maureen	**Otis L.**
1919–1930	10/22/23	1928–	**"Jake" Humphrey**
	Died at birth		1908–1977

CHILDREN

John Joseph	Judith Anne	Joan Marilyn	Thomas Glenn
1935–	1940–	1944–	1945–

Donna Grace Glenn
1915–2005
{ *m. 10/06/1933* }
Otis L. "Jake" Humphrey
1908–1977

CHILDREN

John Joseph	**Judith Anne**	**Joan Marilyn**	**Thomas Glenn**
1935–	1940–	1944–	1945–
{ *m. 1959* }	{ *m. 1959* }	{ *m. 1975* }	{ *m. 1966* }
Janice Hendrix *div.*	Rex F. Kauffman *div.*	Michael F. Lefkow	Patricia Dawson
	{ *m. 1980* }		
	Albert F. Smith		

CHILDREN — CHILDREN — CHILDREN — CHILDREN

Brian Leroy	**Glen Thomas**	**Maria Aithne**	**Monica Joan**
1960–	1963–	1977–	1967–
	{ *m. 1990* }	{ *m. 2006* }	{ *m. 1988* }
Anne Leslie	Elise Samia	Erik Sorensen	Marc Regimbal
1962–			
	CHILDREN		CHILDREN
Michele Leane	*Grant Samuel*	**Helena Claiborne**	*Austin James*
1966–	*1998–*	1979–	*1987–*
{ *1st. m. 1986* }		{ *m. 2005* }	
Russell Burnham *div.*	*Maxwell Alexander*	Jacob Edie	*Vincent Thomas*
	2000–		*1991–*
CHILD			
Kathleen Nicole	*Abigail Rose*	**Laura Bethany**	
1987–	*2006–*	1984–	*Laurel Elizabeth*
			1974–
CHILD		**Margaret Francis**	
Joseph Lee	**Joel Andrew**	1988–	
2007–	1965–		
	{ *m. 1995* }		
{ *2nd. m. 1990* }	**Pamela Dykes**		
Temple Hernlund			
div.	CHILDREN		
	Sarah Rose		
CHILD	*1997–*		
Stephen Tylor	*Elisabeth Margaret*		
1989–	*2000–*		
	John William		
	2002–		

93

JOHN HUMPHREY'S FAMILY:
Front: Anne; Michele Hernlund;
Back: Stephen Hernlund; Ernest Cruz (Anne's fiancé);
John; Katie Burnham; Brian; Lucie Desmarais (friend)

JUDY SMITH'S FAMILY:
Front (children): Elisabeth, Sarah and John Kauffman;
Back: Christopher Kauffman (Judy's stepson); Pam
and Joel Kauffman; Judy; Elise and Glen Kauffman
(Inset: Grant and Max, Glen's children).

JOAN LEFKOW'S FAMILY:
Front: Maria Lefkow Sorensen; Meg; Laura;
Jake Edie (Helena's husband);
Back: Susan; Robert; Joan; Elizabeth; Helena; Frances;
Erik Sorensen (Maria's husband);
(Susan, Robert, Frances and Elizabeth are Joan's in-laws).

TOM HUMPHREY'S FAMILY:
Front: Vincent and Austin Regimbal;
Back: Jason Williamson (Laurel's fiancé);
Laurel; Marc Regimbal (Monica's husband);
Tom; Pat; Monica Regimbal.